THE NINE LIVES OF JOE

A Powerful True Story of Hope & Survival

JOSEPH R. GILBERT

with CALI GILBERT

THE NINE LIVES OF JOE

A Powerful True Story of Hope & Survival

THE NINE LIVES OF JOE

ISBN 9798340459619

Library of Congress Control Number: 2024922995

First printing November, 2024

Serendipity Publishing House
Santa Monica, CA

WWW.TOWER15PRODUCTIONS.COM

Praise for THE NINE LIVES OF JOE

This father-daughter project is all about hope, and the power of resilience and determination. Joe's life experiences remind us that our most challenging obstacles can be our greatest gifts! I also love how the entire book is geared toward supporting the reader in awakening to the lessons and blessings in their own lives. Well done. I highly recommend this!!

Lisa Winston
Intuitive Artist, #1 Best-Selling Author, Inspirational Speaker, and TV Show Host

There is much we can learn from the reflections of another's story and I love the way Joe tells his encouraging story through chapters of his life. What's most powerful is his Greatest Lessons and Blessings at the end of each chapter, and the invitation to do our own reflections. Enjoy the read!

Bobbi DePorter
Author, Cofounder Community Alliance for Youth Success

For Bertha, my loving wife of 53 years.
You remain with me as I embark on this next chapter.

Contents

Introduction

It was November 20, 2023 when I was just wrapping up a beautiful day in San Diego, California. I had spoken to my Dad a couple hours earlier and he shared how it was a good day and my Mom was doing okay, resting peacefully. Then came the phone call I will never forget, the frantic voice on the other end of the line hyperventilating between words. "She's dead", he cried. "Your mother's dead." My heart sank. It was my Dad and he could barely get the words out. I tried to calm him, assuring him to take deep breathes and slowly share what was going on. That moment will live with me forever.

My mother had been ill for years and the pandemic was the final straw. A once vibrant, active woman who was well-known and loved by her neighbors had lost the will to live once she was forced to stay indoors. Little by little her health deteriorated and my father would become a full-time caretaker. Once she passed away I knew it was up to me alone to be there for support and assist my Dad in finding a way to move forward.

Growing up my Dad and I were never really close. We blamed it on the fact that we shared the same birthday and were two stubborn Scorpios who wouldn't budge. We clashed over everything, although there were good times. My Mom and I were even further distant as I never felt seen as an individual. I always felt I was being molded into someone I wasn't, and never allowed to simply be me. When it came to the most memorable moments of my childhood, it was my Dad who was there for emotional support.

As the days passed following my Mom's passing, my Dad

began sharing stories of his life, dating back to his childhood. I was mesmerized by those stories and wanted to learn more. The more he shared, the more I realized that I wanted to share these stories in a book. We had spent twenty-five years apart after I left home and moved out on my own, first to New York and then to California. There was a lot I didn't know about my father, why he behaved the way he did when I was young and why we never got along.

After he began sharing his story, especially from his youth, I began to see my father in a new light. I began to realize he was simply doing the best he could with what he had been taught growing up. I realized that ever since he was a young boy, all he ever sought was love and acknowledgement for his achievements. These things he never received from those closest to him, he continued to long for as an adult.

The more I learned, the more I gained a whole new respect for the man who brought me into this world. The more I learned, the more I realized that our similarities were our greatest strengths and by embracing those similarities and also appreciating our differences, we could create something amazing together.

I hope you enjoy this story we are sharing together, and I hope it inspires you to live life to the absolute fullest. None of us really know how much time we have on this planet, but each of us has the choice to make this life the best it can be.

Cali Gilbert, *Daughter of Joseph Gilbert*

Life #1   THE LITTLE BOY

It seemed my life was already pre-destined when I entered the world in 1940. I arrived sooner than expected and I was certainly not planned. It also automatically built in the instinct of never being late. I learned very early on that if I were to survive, I needed to rely on myself and no one else. I never really knew my father who was married with another family when I was conceived. All I was told was that he was a military man who served in World War II as part of the Army/Air Force.

I was born in Fredericksburg, Virginia but my mother moved us to Baltimore, Maryland when I was two years old. She worked at Martin State Airport which played an active role in the production of military aircraft and their components. The war had begun a year prior to my birth and lasted six years. It began with Germany's invasion of Poland led by Adolf Hitler in September, 1939. By the time I entered the world, Germany was in a heavy battle with Great Britain. A year later, the infamous battle of Pearl Harbor took place when Japanese aircraft attacked the U.S. Pacific Fleet in the Hawaiian Islands. More than twenty-five hundred Americans were killed. Days after the attacks on Pearl Harbor, Hitler declared war on the United States. This was the world I would be introduced to, and it wouldn't be the last time I experienced a world at war.

Those early years I don't really remember much. What I do remember is we moved around a lot. I felt like a gypsy and there was never much stability in my life. As my fifth birthday approached, the big headline in the news was the threat of nuclear weapons with Germany, Russia, and Japan at the center of attention. On August 6, 1945 the first atomic bomb was dropped on Hiroshima. Nearly eighty thousand people died and another ninety thousand were injured. Three days later another bomb dropped on Nagasaki resulting in a similar fate. Japan would soon surrender and the war would finally come to an end.

The war must have had a negative impact on my father because soon after he returned, my parents decided to go their separate ways. Age five is a year that vividly remains with me to this day. As my mother worked, I was often left with people she knew, and let's just say I wasn't really monitored when it came to my actions. I often had to find ways to entertain myself. During one particular time I was being looked after by a couple who had a German Shephard. I was unsupervised and spotted a calendar that I was eager to retrieve. As I stepped over the dog's water and food bowls, the dog spotted me and must have thought I was going after its food because it lunged right at me. With teeth snarling, it came right at my head and took a bite. I must have blacked out as I was told it was touch and go for a while as I almost bled out.

Somehow I recovered from that ordeal, but not four months later I was hit by a car while playing good-guys, bad-guys with some friends. We were playing in the yard that led out to an alley.

I was chasing someone and jumped out into the alley and yelled, "GOTCHA!" Next thing I knew the car was on top of me. It took out my knees and the hood ornament caught my chin slicing it open. Somehow I survived that as well, but each time, according to my mother, it was my fault.

A year after the war ended my mother would remarry and we moved again. We would continue to move around to different apartments throughout Baltimore. Sometimes we would share a place with my grandparents which was nice. I have good memories of them when I was young. They were old school, from the country, and cooked everything from scratch. Being from Virginia, everything was fresh. At age seven, I began going to Sunday school. Mom never went with me. She'd give me two dollars for the church collection. I'd put it all in the collection except for twenty cents. With that I would go to the bakery across the street and buy an éclair for ten cents. The remaining ten cents went towards the trolley to take me home.

At age eight I began working taking odd jobs such as delivering groceries, cutting grass, selling newspapers, and shoveling snow. I did a little bit of everything. I knew if I ever wanted anything I would have to pay for it myself so I earned every bit of it. At age nine I did ask for something I really wanted. One of my Mom's relatives had a piano and whenever we would visit I would play around with the keys. I asked Mom if I could take lessons. At first she obliged, but after three lessons she claimed it was too expensive and I wasn't able to go back.

My first decade ended pretty much the same way it began, in the hospital. While at home I began experiencing abdominal pain. It became so intense that I was rushed to emergency where it was determined my appendix was about to burst. Luckily I made it in time and had it removed. How I survived Life #1 is beyond me. Between the accidents and feeling neglected, it was a decade filled with lessons for a young child who simply wanted to be loved.

Greatest lesson from Life #1

I can't depend on anyone but myself.

Greatest blessing from Life #1

I became independent.

REFLECTION

1. Think back to your life between your birth through age nine. Can you recall any significant moments?

_____

_____

_____

_____

_____

2. What lessons did you learn from those experiences?

_____

_____

_____

_____

_____

3. What blessings did you receive from those experiences?

_____

_____

_____

_____

_____

4. Who was the most important person in your life at that time?

_____

_____

_____

_____

_____

5. What did you learn from them?

_____

_____

_____

_____

_____

6. Do you have someone in your life now who is that age whom you can support or mentor?

_____

_____

_____

_____

_____

7. How can you pay forward the lessons that you learned during that time?

_____

_____

_____

_____

_____

Life#2 THE BOY BECOMES A MAN

Life #2 began pretty much the same way as the first, with war. The Korean War broke out not long before my tenth birthday in June, 1950. It was a war between North and South Korea and their allies. North Korea was supported by the People's Republic of China and the Soviet Union and South Korea by the United Nations led by the United States. It would last some three years.

Life #2 is where I feel I learned the most that would be pivotal to adulthood. I attended public school but found what brought me the most joy were the classes where we had to create something using our hands. It was also the place where I would make the most friends. That was nice as it got me out of the house and I didn't feel so alone. At age eleven I took my first job at a neighborhood Jewish grocery store. The owner was really nice and offered me fifty cents an hour to stock shelves, and a free lunch. To an eleven-year-old, that was a great deal. I worked at that store until I was fourteen years old. I would take my pay and go bowling with my friends as I grew older.

The accidents also continued as I grew older but some of them weren't my fault at all. At age eleven while I was being looked after by another couple my Mom knew, we visited a candy shop. The selection of candy was vast and I couldn't make up my mind when asked what I'd like. The man looking after me told me I was taking too long. Suddenly I felt this shove in my back and I went flying head first into the glass case containing the candy. I broke my nose and had a bloody face. Yet once again, I was made to believe it was my fault.

Those preadolescence years were certainly defining. My relationship with my mother was strained because I felt my emotional needs were not being met. I hesitated to ask her for anything because I began to realize the answer would always be no. I remember asking her for a bike so I wouldn't have to walk everywhere and my friends had bikes. My stepfather however, thought I should have one so he built one for me out of scraps he found at the junkyard. I loved that bike and really enjoyed riding it. I also got another dog, Inky at age eleven. I loved that dog and he was my best friend. He was such a good dog and well-trained. I wanted to keep him indoors but Mom wouldn't let me, so I built him a dog house in the yard. My previous dog, Snowball was tiny and I loved him as well, but someone stole him right out of our yard.

Having a male father figure care was something I hadn't experienced in my early years, so I was grateful for the time we had together even if it was short-lived. Shortly before my twelfth birthday he was called away to the Korean War. He was a member of the Merchant Marines but then joined the Navy. During the war he was aboard one of the Destroyers that served as support for the aircraft carriers in the South China Sea. He would be gone for two years.

My teen years began in the Baltimore neighborhood of Waverly near Memorial Stadium. I enjoyed living there as I was able to watch the construction of the second deck of seats prior to the 1954 season. The Baltimore Orioles would begin their first season at Memorial Stadium in 1954, yet their franchise's history stems back to the original Milwaukee Brewers of the Western League in 1894 followed by the St. Louis Browns in 1902 when the team moved to St. Louis.

During the time my stepfather was gone my Mom carried on with other men. It made me angry because I couldn't understand how she could behave that way when her husband was off serving his country. After the eighth grade I had had enough of school and I ended up spending time with the wrong crowd and getting into trouble simply by being in the wrong place at that wrong time. Finally at age fourteen I had had enough of the revolving door of strange men and decided to run away. I hitchhiked all the way to North Carolina thumbing rides with truck drivers. Mom called the police and they came after me and took me back to Baltimore. Mom had had enough and decided to send me to reform school for a year. It was jail as you couldn't go anywhere, and I hated it as it was in the middle of nowhere.

Just weeks prior to my fifteenth birthday, the Vietnam War broke out. Like the Korean War, it was fought between North Vietnam and South Vietnam. The North was supported by China and the Soviet Union, while the South by the United States and its anti-communist allies. Unlike the war in Korea, the Vietnam War would last some twenty years, and as a teenager I certainly didn't expect to be right in the thick of it a decade later. Once I was able to come home after being at reform school, it was baseball that occupied most of my time. I really enjoyed playing with my friends. I loved the game and I batted right-handed and threw left-handed. At the end of the 1955 season, the Baltimore Orioles called up an eighteen-year-old third baseman named Brooks

Robinson. He was only a few years older than I was and soon became my favorite player.

During the 1956 season I had a great opportunity to watch the game up close as I landed a job at Memorial Stadium selling popcorn. It was great as I got to watch the games for free and make some extra money. Brooks Robinson spent most of the 1956 season in the Orioles minor league system, but they did call him up in September which was great. He only played in fifteen games, but there was one six-game home stand where I got to watch him play. 1956 was also an exciting year for our football team, The Baltimore Colts, who also played at Memorial Stadium. They brought in a new quarterback named Johnny Unitas who had been drafted by the Pittsburgh Steelers the previous year. I really enjoyed watching him play as well, even though he had a rocky start.

At age sixteen when my friends were getting their drivers licenses, I wasn't allow to as my Mom didn't want me driving. She was afraid I'd wreck the car. So I continued to rely on my bike and public transportation to get around town. I didn't end up getting my license until age thirty-two after I was married and we had our first child. It had become a necessity at that point. Also at age sixteen I decided to go on another adventure crossing state lines. My friend and I decided to hitchhike to Tennessee. We had fun but this time we decided to return home. By this point it seemed my Mom stopped caring where I went as long as I stayed out of trouble.

The accidents continued which really wasn't a surprise. Once when I was playing baseball at age seventeen, I was the pitcher. The batter came up and I threw the ball. In a split second he hit it right back at me and it caught me between the eyes. Then another time that same year I was spending time with friends as a local pool. There was a slide and I was showing off for the girls. Everyone was sliding down feet first but I decided it would be cool to go head first. Just as I reached the bottom of the slide, I turned my head and my face struck the edge. I ended up breaking my nose for the second time.

At age eighteen it was all about football in Baltimore as the Colts were playing in the NFL Championship Game. My favorite player, Johnny Unitas was the reigning MVP after a stellar 1957 season. The game was played on December 28, 1958 at Yankee Stadium in New York City between the Colts and the New York Giants. It was the first NFL playoff game to be decided in sudden death overtime with the Colts winning 23-17. Soon it would be considered, "The Greatest Game Ever Played".

My late teen years were spent with friends with sports and music as the focal points of my life. I really enjoyed music and not just playing instruments whenever I'd get a chance, but also singing. We'd go to restaurants that had bands playing and I'd get up there and start singing. I also sang in the church choir for years which I really enjoyed. I also got a job with another Jewish grocery store which I really enjoyed. The owner was a really nice older man and when he retired he gave me his wooden Indiana cash drawer along with rolls of price stickers. To this day I still have the wooden cash drawers and use them for my art proceeds. The bell still rings when you open it up after all this time.

I had my share of girlfriends, but nothing serious until I was nineteen years old. That's when I met a fellow artist and she was amazing. She was so talented and we really hit it off, but she was only fifteen at the time. We still spent as much time together as we could and really enjoyed our time together. Yet it was difficult to imagine what a solid relationship looked like since I didn't have the best role model.

Greatest lesson from Life #2

If I wanted anything in life I needed to work hard to obtain it myself.

Greatest blessing from Life #2

Became self-reliant.

REFLECTION

1. Think back to your life between ages ten through nineteen. Can you recall any significant moments?

_____

_____

_____

_____

_____

2. What lessons did you learn from those experiences?

_____

_____

_____

_____

_____

3. What blessings did you receive from those experiences?

_____

_____

_____

_____

_____

4. Who was the most important person in your life at that time?

_____

_____

_____

_____

_____

5. What did you learn from them?

_____

_____

_____

_____

_____

6. Do you have someone in your life now who is that age whom you can support or mentor?

_____

_____

_____

_____

_____

7. How can you pay forward the lessons that you learned during that time?

_____

_____

_____

_____

_____

*Life#*3 THE HARSH ROAD TO LOVE

Life #3 began with the Vietnam War still raging and the Civil Rights Movement was headlining the country, especially in Baltimore where we saw several student sit-ins. Morgan State College led one of the biggest and had a history of civil rights activism. Their focus was on department stores, and the restaurants inside them, which continued to be very segregated. Lasting three weeks, the students were successful in getting the department store restaurants to change their policies.

Music continued to play a large part in my life into my twenties, and I had a very defining moment in my twentieth year. I had been singing with the church choir when someone saw me sing. I was invited to apply for a scholarship with the Peabody Institute, the top music conservatory at Johns Hopkins University. I decided to try out and I came in first for tenors. I was offered the scholarship, but when I told Mom she thought the whole idea was ridiculous and said it would be a waste of time, so I never moved forward. Looking back now I should have just gone ahead without her blessing, but at the time it was just another blow to my confidence. In the summer of 1961 I had a big decision to make. The girl I had been seeing was graduating from high school and would leave for college. As much as I wanted to be with her, I also didn't want to hold her back. Before we parted ways she gave me two of her drawings, one a blue jay and the other a cardinal. She signed both and I still have them hanging in my home all these years later. I would see her once more many years later when her father passed away. She was married and had two children. I wanted to reconnect, but her Mom suggested we just leave things as they were as she had moved on, so I obliged.

The early sixties in Baltimore saw a lot of growth in some areas and a lot of change in others. The white population was moving from the City to the suburbs with downtown and surrounding areas being replaced by African American families. The Baltimore Beltway which had been under construction since 1955 was finally completed. It was the first beltway within the United States to be part of the Interstate Highway System. It connected the City to the suburbs intersecting with Maryland Route 2 and US Route 40. This was also the time when I ventured out and got my own apartment. These were pretty mellow years where I worked in construction and stayed pretty much to myself.

In November, 1966 I joined the Army as a way of getting away from my Mom. Our relationship continued to be strained yet I still cared about her. I had no idea what to really expect, but certainly not what I was faced with. Right off the bat it was anything but dull. Four weeks into basic training I completely shattered my right knee. I had to undergo surgery where they basically took my knee out, put it back together and placed it back. I spent six months in a military hospital recovering from that ordeal. When I was finally released from the hospital I was still having issues with my knee but I had to go through basic training again. This time I made it through finishing in the top two of my class. The reward, my orders for Vietnam. It was ironic really because of the class of forty-eight students, most were sent to Germany, but I and the guy who finished atop the class were sent to Vietnam.

I would spend eighteen months in Vietnam from October, 1967 to June of 1969. I was part of the Fifth Battalion, Second Artillery in support of the 9th Infantry based at Bien Hoa Air Base, north of Saigon. The 9th Infantry Division was tasked with defending the Mekong Delta from the Viet Cong. It was deemed with protecting the local population, and supporting the South Vietnamese government. We were stationed right in the heart of the battle in the Mekong Delta, a vast area in Southern Vietnam made up of rivers, swamps and islands. This was a crucial area and home to forty percent of the Southern Vietnam population. It was also the area that produced most of the country's rice crop. The Viet Cong would use this area for attacks and to harass water traffic. It was our job to support the 9th Infantry in protecting the local communities.

On January 31, 1968 a surprise attack on South Vietnam caught the Mobile Riverine Force (MRF) off guard. The MRF was an Army/Navy force responsible for keeping the rivers in the delta open and safe for shipping. Our 9th Infantry was part of that force, and it was our responsibility to provide support for them where needed. Code named, the Tet Offensive after the Vietnamese New Year holiday, it proved to be a major escalation in the war and one of the largest military campaigns. During that time I saw and experienced things I wouldn't wish on my worst enemy, and was haunted by that time upon my return home.

When I processed out in Oakland, California in 1969 I felt as though I were at a crossroads. I knew there was nothing waiting for me back home, so I wondered if I should just stay in California and begin a new life there. I decided to flip a coin. Heads I stay, tails I go back. I looked down at the coin and it was tails. Being back in Baltimore felt strange. There was no welcome home party. There wasn't a job waiting for me when I returned. There wasn't anything and I soon became depressed, wondering why I bothered to come back.

On November 8th one of my buddies saw that I was feeling down and suggested we go to Sweeney's, a neighborhood cocktail lounge. I didn't really want to go out but he insisted so I figured why not? It was a Saturday night and the place was packed. I walked in with my friends and noticed there weren't any places to sit except two stools side by side at the bar. I walked over and sat down, just as this young lady did the same. Her name was Bertha and she was there with friends of her own. We looked at one another and I said, "Can you believe it? Seems like we got the last seats". Just then the bartender walked over and said that the band would be taking a break and they were putting on the jukebox. All of the sudden, Frank Sinatra's, *Strangers in the Night* came on. I looked over and asked Bertha if she would like to dance and she took my hand. Before leaving that night I asked her for her number. She wrote a message instead on the piece of paper. The problem was that it was all in Spanish and I couldn't understand a word of it. I nearly threw the piece of paper away when I got home, but luckily I turned it over to find her name and number. I called her the next day and we decided to go on our first date on November 19th which happened to be my birthday. I suppose I knew right away that this was the woman I wanted to spend the rest of my life with.

Bertha was from Peru and was working for a doctor in Maryland. She was on the verge of going back to Peru when we met. We ended up spending Thanksgiving together with the family she worked for. They took to me fondly and I to them. Before she headed home for Christmas, I purchased a ring and proposed marriage. She accepted and was excited to share the news with her parents. While she was away, I decided to paint something for her. I painted the Blue Boy by Thomas Gainsborough and had it framed for her. I was about to embark on a brand new chapter in my life and had no idea what the future would hold. All I knew was that I had found the person I wanted to share that life with.

Greatest lesson from Life #3

I had more strength than I gave myself credit for.

Greatest blessing from Life #3

I found the love of my life.

REFLECTION

1. Think back to your life between ages twenty through twenty-nine. Can you recall any significant moments?

_____

_____

_____

_____

_____

2. What lessons did you learn from those experiences?

_____

_____

_____

_____

_____

3. What blessings did you receive from those experiences?

_____

_____

_____

_____

_____

4. Who was the most important person in your life at that
    time?

_____

_____

_____

_____

_____

5. What did you learn from them?

_____

_____

_____

_____

_____

6. Do you have someone in your life now who is that age whom you can support or mentor?

_____

_____

_____

_____

_____

7. How can you pay forward the lessons that you learned during that time?

_____

_____

_____

_____

_____

8. If you ARE this age now, what lessons from your past can you implement into your life now?

_____

_____

_____

_____

_____

Life#4 A WHOLE NEW WORLD

Life #4 began with preparing for our wedding. The doctor Bertha worked for had a wonderful family and they lived in a beautiful large home in Owings Mills, a neighborhood in northern Baltimore County. They offered to take care of all the arrangements for the wedding which would take place at the end of May in 1970. Bertha was Catholic so we married in a church ceremony near Owings Mills. It was a very nice ceremony, but one that was delayed slightly as no one could find the bride. In the spring of 1970 Baltimore was invaded by the Brood X cicadas after spending seventeen years underground. They were everywhere and Bertha was absolutely captivated by these flying creatures she had never seen before. While the wedding hymn began and I was standing at the head of the isle awaiting her appearance, she was outside by the trees counting cicadas. We had to send someone out to find her. This was a story that never grew old and always brought laughs to whomever we shared it with many years later. The reception took place at the doctor's home as we were surrounded by friends and loved ones.

On my thirtieth birthday in November we welcomed our first child, a girl we named Carol Lea (Cali). Like me, my birthday baby was early as she wasn't due until December. We lived in an apartment about three miles east of Memorial Stadium and next door to Mom. She was a big help in lending a hand while I worked to support my new family. Sports was all the talk around Baltimore at the end of 1970 and beginning of 1971. A few weeks before my birthday baby arrived, the Orioles won the World Series four games to one over Sparky Anderson's Cincinnati Reds. My hero, Brooks Robinson was named Most Valuable Player hitting .429 with seventeen total bases, breaking the record for a five-game series. The victory was a bit of redemption for the Orioles who had lost to the New York Mets the year prior.

In January, 1971 the Baltimore Colts won their first Super Bowl over the Dallas Cowboys. The Colts had an 11-2 record to win their first AFC East title. The Colts offensive backfield coach, Don McCafferty had taken over the Head Coaching position after Don Shula departed in February 1970 after seven seasons to coach Miami Dolphins. Between the Orioles winning the World Series and the Colts the Super Bowl, the buzz around Baltimore was electric.

The following year however, things took a turn for the Baltimore Colts. Owner, Carroll Rosenbloom, citing friction with the City of Baltimore and the local press, decided to trade the franchise to Robert Irsay and received the Los Angeles Rams in return. Sadly, under the new management, the Colts didn't reach the postseason for three consecutive years following their Super Bowl victory. The biggest heartache came when they traded my favorite player, Johnny Unitas to the San Diego Chargers.

After a few years in our first apartment we decided to move into a more modern apartment in Parkville another three miles north of where we had been. I also decided to pursue my art by taking classes at a Commercial Art School. It was there where I met two of my mentors, Mary and Craig who encouraged me to tap into what was inside of me when creating art. I really enjoyed my time there and I learned a lot. I also met a lot of new people and made new friends. It was there where I met the husband of a fellow student who was an Air Force recruiter. We had a long talk about my military experience and he encouraged me to join the Air Force Reserve.

In 1975 I was working the nightshift at Dorman's Electric on Lexington Street in Baltimore. Joining the Air Force Reserve and working weekends at Andrews Air Force Base would bring in extra money which we could certainly use at the time with a growing family. 1976 was a big year for our family. After spending my entire life living in apartments and boarding houses, I wanted something better for my family. I wanted to buy a house. Our family was also growing as we welcomed our second child, a son we named Eric Jonathan in September. Bertha and I looked for a new home in various neighborhoods around Baltimore City when we finally came across a property in Hampden, an area whose history dated back to the end of the Civil War with the construction of the cotton mills and the housing for their workers.

From the early 1800s to the early 1900s, the areas of Hampden and Woodbury contained eight cotton mills and a foundry along the Jones Falls, a river that flows through Baltimore and into the Inner Harbor. A group of stone and frame houses lined the streets east of the river. That is where we found our new home. It was a frame house that was in the process of being remodeled and therefore in our price range as first-time homeowners. At first Bertha wasn't crazy about the house as the top floor needed work.

The drywall was still bare, but the bones of the house were great. I saw the potential of what it could be and therefore I was excited about moving our family in towards the end of 1977. We ended up paying twelve thousand dollars and paid it off in eight years.

The latter part of the seventies were spent settling into our new home and I looking after my young family. Cali wasn't thrilled about the new house coming from a modern apartment, but I did my best to assure her it would look nice after we fixed it up. Our new neighborhood provided new opportunities and one I could share with Cali. She became interested in ice skating after watching Dorothy Hamill win Gold during the Winter Olympic Games which took place in Innsbruck, Austria. We had a local rink not far from the house so I decided to take her to a public session. I got out on the ice with her, and even though I was pretty wobbly and had to hold on to the edge the entire time, Cali had the best time.

It was a bit challenging for Cali with the new home and also not being the center of attention with a little brother now taking up most of our attention at home. She also began to voice her opinion and act out if things didn't quite go her way. I'll never forget one particular incident that scared the life out of me. Cali was born left-handed, as was my son, Eric. Yet my wife felt left out as she was right-handed. She began to take everything out of Cali's left hand and place it into her right-hand so that she would become more dominant using her right hand. She even learned to write with her right hand.

Well, on this particular day, Cali rebelled. She didn't want to do her homework so we decided to lock her outside on the back porch until she settled down and gave in. Well, she had another idea all together. She took her right hand and made a fist and put it through the paned-glass window of the back door. She stood there in her school uniform with blood pouring out of her hand, her blue uniform stained with blood. She looked us both in the eye and said, "Now look what you made me do." Frantically, I grabbed a large towel, placed it around her hand and picked her up rushing to the car. My wife and I headed straight for the closest hospital rushing past the red lights. When we arrived, Cali was rushed into the emergency room where the doctor cleaned up the wound and stitched her up. She laughed and said the stitches tickled. I was a wreck. She would return to school with her right hand all bandaged up and forced to use her left hand to write. Guess she showed us. Today she continues to write with her right hand, but does everything else with her left, so the gift came in the fact that she's now ambidextrous.

Greatest lesson from Life #4

With hard work and determination, I can create a life I love.

Greatest blessing from Life #4

A loving family.

REFLECTION

1. Think back to your life between ages thirty through thirty-nine. Can you recall any significant moments?

_____

_____

_____

_____

_____

2. What lessons did you learn from those experiences?

_____

_____

_____

_____

_____

3. What blessings did you receive from those experiences?

_____

_____

_____

_____

_____

4. Who was the most important person in your life at that time?

_____

_____

_____

_____

_____

5. What did you learn from them?

_____

_____

_____

_____

_____

6. Do you have someone in your life now who is that age whom you can support or mentor?

_____

_____

_____

_____

_____

7. How can you pay forward the lessons that you learned during that time?

_____

_____

_____

_____

_____

8. If you ARE this age now, what lessons from your past can you implement into your life now?

_____

_____

_____

_____

_____

Life #5 THE LOVE OF THE GAME COMES FULL CIRCLE

Life #5 welcomed in the decade of the eighties which was filled with innovation in Baltimore. The introduction of Harborplace in downtown in the summer of 1980 featured a new area surrounding the inner harbor. It invited not only Baltimoreans, but tourist alike to the center of the City. It was a wonderful place to go as a family to visit the Science Center, National Aquarium and Rash Field. Restaurants and shops lined the harbor and it was a wonderful place to walk and spend an afternoon.

This was also a time where I got to watch a generation come full circle. Ever since I was a boy, baseball has been a huge influence in my life and some of my greatest role models came from baseball and other sports. I also suppose the love of the game came from my grandfather who was a huge sport enthusiast. He loved all sports and on some days you could find him watching a game and listening to another one on the radio simultaneously. I suppose while raising my daughter, Cali, that love of the game was passed down to the next generation.

Around age ten, Cali became friends with another girl who also loved baseball and before long she was asking me to take her to see a live game at Memorial Stadium. That day would finally come in May, 1983. My hero, Brooks Robinson had retired six years prior in August, 1977, but a young shortstop named Cal Ripken, Jr. had emerged as the next great homegrown talent. Ripken grew up around baseball as his father Cal Ripken, Sr. was a player and coach within the Orioles organization. In August, 1982 he was called up to the Major Leagues as a third baseman who would eventually transition to becoming an everyday shortstop and nicknamed, "The Iron Man" due to his consecutive game streak.

Well, little did I know that by taking Cali to her first game in the spring of 1983, that one chance encounter would change everything. The Orioles were facing the Oakland A's at Memorial Stadium on a Friday night. Cali wanted to go down to the dugout to see if she could get Cal to sign her autograph book. He came over and signed her book and was very kind. The Orioles won that game 9-2 and Cal hit two homeruns and had four RBI to top it off. We and the large crowd of over forty-four thousand were thrilled. From that day on, Cali had her own baseball hero.

Just as Brooks Robinson had become a role model for me in my teenage years, Cal would do the same for my daughter during hers. They soon became friends and he would be there for all the significant moments of her life, from graduating grade school, to getting her driver's license, to graduating college. He treated her like a little sister and made a point of sharing what he called, the "stages of life" with her when she rebelled against anything I or my wife would share. Cali and I really struggled in maintaining a close relationship during those teen years as I couldn't give her the attention I once had now that we had another child and I was away on the weekends. Luckily she had someone who she admired and who could instill those lessons she needed to learn as a growing young lady.

In October, 1983 the Orioles would go all the way to the World Series where they would face the Philadelphia Phillies who were based just up Interstate 95. It was the first World Series where the two teams didn't use air travel since they were so close to one another. The Orioles were led by first-year manager, Joe Altobelli who took over after legendary manager, Earl Weaver retired after sixteen years. The offense was led by Eddie Murray and Cal Ripken Jr. Cal would win the 1983 MVP award that year as well. The Orioles would win the series four games to one and be crowned World Series Champions. Following the victory, we along with some of our neighboring friends headed to Memorial Stadium to await the team's arrival from Philadelphia. It was an incredible environment as everyone came with signs and cheering. We had a blast. The following day the City of Baltimore celebrated with a fabulous parade to honor the team. It was a time that we'll always remember fondly.

In March, 1984 football fans in Baltimore were dealt with a harsh blow as our beloved Baltimore Colts left town in the middle of the night to move to Indianapolis. We wouldn't find out until the next day what had happened. Apparently, the team was under the threat of eminent domain from the City of Baltimore, so they packed everything up into a number of Mayflower moving trucks and skipped town in the middle of the night in a snowstorm nonetheless. It felt like such a betrayal to us fans who loved the team.

The following month we received some surprise news in the form of a Sports Illustrated magazine. The cover of the magazine had Yogi Berra on the cover and inside a multi-page feature on Cal Ripken, Jr. There were a number of photographs that accompanied the article and in one Cal was signing autographs for a group of fans. Right front and center of those receiving an autograph were my kids, Cali and Eric. My wife was so excited that she grabbed the magazine and went straight to their school to share the news. The children, now 13 and 7 were called to the Principal's Office where my wife and the Principal relayed the big news. All of the sudden my kids were instant celebrities. Eric was a bit young to fully understand what was happening, but Cali ate it up and signed her first autograph shortly after when someone recognized her from the magazine.

When Cali began high school, she attended a private school not far from Memorial Stadium, so that became her second home. Back in those days we didn't mind leaving her alone with her friends. She would go to school and if there was a game being played that night, they'd go straight to the ballpark after school. We'd then pick her up after the game or she got a ride from one of our friends. Eric's interest were in action figures and Star Wars. He also grew to love baseball and played Little League.

Those early years of the 1980s were focused on family and sports and bridging the two together. The second half of the decade brought about heartbreaking news out of the space program. On January 28, 1986 the Space Shuttle Challenger broke apart shortly after take-off and killing all the crew members aboard just off the coast of Florida. It was the first fatal accident involving an American spacecraft. It was heartbreaking not only for the loss of life, but because of the impact it had on the youth of our country. The mission introduced the Teacher in Space Program and teacher, Christa McAuliffe was one of the perished.

Due to the program and media interest, the launch and disaster were broadcasted live in schools across the country leaving a chilling impact on all those who watched.

In May, 1986 we came together as a country in hopes of raising funds for the fight against hunger and homelessness. Nearly six million people linked hands between New York City to Long Beach, California. People were encouraged to donate ten dollars in order to join the chain. The event raised about fifteen million for charities, far less than anticipated, but at least many did their part to help those experiencing homelessness.

1988 was a special year as Cali graduated from high school and my father-in-law, Jose came to visit from Peru. It was wonderful to have him here and Bertha was thrilled to be able to have this time with her father. It was difficult at times for her as she came from a large family, yet they were all back in Peru. She had nine siblings. Luckily she was very close to the family of the doctor she worked for and they became her extended family. My mother also had many siblings who lived either here in Maryland or in Virginia, so it was nice to be able to spend time together and have our children get to know their cousins.

We wrapped up the decade with Cali beginning her first year of college at a private school here in Maryland. She wasn't thrilled to attend as she wanted to continue skating and didn't have an interest in academics at that time, yet we knew it was important that she had a good education. Eric was wrapping up his final years in elementary school and would soon begin a new chapter in his life. Our focus was on family and trying to spend as much time together as we could.

Greatest lesson from Life #5

Community and friends are very important.

Greatest blessing from Life #5

Great friends

REFLECTION

1. Think back to your life between ages forty through forty-nine. Can you recall any significant moments?

_____

_____

_____

_____

_____

2. What lessons did you learn from those experiences?

_____

_____

_____

_____

_____

3. What blessings did you receive from those experiences?

_____

_____

_____

_____

_____

4. Who was the most important person in your life at that time?

_____

_____

_____

_____

_____

5. What did you learn from them?

_____

_____

_____

_____

_____

6. Do you have someone in your life now who is that age whom you can support or mentor?

_____

_____

_____

_____

_____

7. How can you pay forward the lessons that you learned during that time?

_____

_____

_____

_____

_____

8. If you ARE this age now, what lessons from your past can you implement into your life now?

_____

_____

_____

_____

_____

Life #6 THE WORLD IN CRISIS

Life #6 began with significant world news coming out of Germany with the tearing down of the Berlin Wall the separated East and West Germany. The opening of the Brandenburg Gate came at the end of 1989 and demolition of the wall began in June, 1990. This was such a significant event as the wall stood since the early 1960s. The celebrations from both sides flashed across our television screens and headlined the world news.

Sadly, the 1990s also began pretty much the same way other decades of my life had begun, with a war. The Gulf War broke out in August, 1990 between Iraq and a coalition of forty-two countries led by the United States. The defense was carried out in two phases, Operation Desert Shield between August, 1990 and January, 1991 which entailed the military buildup for the operation. The second wave which involved an aerial bombing campaign against Iraq was labeled Operation Desert Storm and took place between January, 1991 and February 28 with the American-led liberation of Kuwait.

In late January I was called to active duty with the United State Air Force and we were sent to Upper Heyford, England as part of the support team for the medical squadron. We spent five weeks there. We then returned to the United States where I would spend the next eleven weeks at Andrews Air Force Base in Maryland. Those months away were challenging for my wife as she was left with a teenage son and home to run. Cali was twenty by this point and able to take care of herself. She was there as much as she could be to support her mother, but it wasn't the same as me being there.

When I did return home we tried to spend as much time as we could as a family and traveled often as well. We spent quite a bit of time in Canada as Cali had been skating there for some years. We really enjoyed spending time there and the drive up from Maryland was beautiful. We especially loved spending time around the Thousand Islands region that spans the border of the United States in Canada. Instead of crossing New York State on our drives up and back, we would take Interstate 81 all the way up to Canada and then cross Ontario. It was always an adventure that we really enjoyed as a family.

At the end of 1991 I endured another health scare when a blood clot in my leg made its way up to my lung and I had trouble breathing. I was rushed to the emergency room and luckily the doctors were able to intervene in time to save my life. From that day on I've been on blood thinner medication. When I look back on my life now I realize that despite all the health scares, I never gave up. Somehow I got stronger with each challenge and it made me realize just how much I was capable of handling. With each challenge, my resilience grew.

The next few years were focused on strengthening my relationship with my family as my military career came to an end in 1992. I had given my twenty years and was now eligible to receive a pension. I realized the time away from home had put a strain on my relationships, so I wanted to do what I could to mend things. Also, Cali had been focused on life in Canada and even had moved on from being an Orioles fan. In 1985 she began following the Toronto Blue Jays and the last couple of years was thrilled when the Jays won back to back World Series titles in 1991 and 1992. Luckily my son, Eric remained loyal to the Orioles so I still had someone to cheer on the team with. I'll admit it was a bit different however with the Orioles moving into their new stadium, Oriole Park at Camden Yards in downtown Baltimore. After watching them build Memorial Stadium as a teenager, it broke my heart when they began the demolition of the stadium a decade later.

1994 was an interesting year for sports in Baltimore. The Orioles played well and ended up second in the American League East behind the New York Yankees, although the season was cut short. On August 12th the players decided to strike since an agreement could not be reached between the Players Association and the Owners. The issue was over a salary cap the owners wanted to impose and a revenue sharing agreement. When all was said and done, the last two months of the season as well as the entire playoffs were wiped out. It was the first time the World Series was not played since 1904.

The strike left a bad taste in the mouths of fans as the bickering over money continued. The good news came in the form of expansion football and from no other place but north of the border. The Canadian Football League decided to expand with five American teams and one just happened to come to Baltimore. The Baltimore Stallions as they were nicknamed played two seasons at Memorial Stadium, 1994 and 1995. They reached the Grey Cup Championship game both times, losing to the B.C.

Lions in 1994 and defeating the Calgary Stampeders 37-20 the following year to become the first American team to hold claim to the Grey Cup. Cali really enjoyed having the Stallions in town as she was spending a lot of time in Canada and understood the game. She had the opportunity to meet the team during their Championship runs and came away with some great memorabilia. It was also nice to have a reason to visit Memorial Stadium since the Orioles were now playing at their new stadium downtown.

April, 1995 was a time of disappointment that the baseball strike still remained at an impasse, and then things became scary with the bombing in Oklahoma City. Former Army veteran Timothy McVeigh and his co-conspirator, Terry Nichols were the masterminds behind the bombing of the Alfred P. Murrah Federal Building that killed 167 people and injured nearly seven hundred. The events in Oklahoma City remain the deadliest act of domestic terrorism in U.S. history.

The second half of the nineties brought heartbreaking news from across the pond. First came the shocking death in August, 1997 of Princess Diana in Paris after being chased through the streets by the paparazzi. Then within the same week at the beginning of September came the news of the passing of Mother Teresa in India. Two prominent women in the world who stood for love and compassion, gone. My wife had several friends living in England at the time so the news of Diana was huge. We had followed the Royal Family for years and it was devastating news, especially knowing she had two young children. My wife also took the news of Mother Teresa's death pretty hard being a devout Catholic.

Life on the home front was changing as well. Cali had a life of her own and worked in publishing, and our son Eric was now also an adult with his own life. In June, 1998 Cali decided to spend the summer in Europe as her work schedule allowed for the flexibility. Later that year the big news here in the U.S. was John Glenn becoming the oldest person to fly in space as he took part in the Space Shuttle Discovery's mission. He was seventy-seven years old and the mission lasted nine days.

1998 came to an abrupt close with the impeachment of President Bill Clinton due to the Monica Lewinsky scandal. He was later acquitted, but his reputation tarnished. During the same time the United States along with the United Kingdom bombed Iraq who failed to comply with the United Nations Security Council. The big issue was Iraq's interference with United Nations Inspectors who were searching for potential weapons of mass destruction.

Disgusted by the political drama and war on the verge of breaking out again, Cali had had enough of the U.S and decided to move to bordering Niagara Falls to make the journey to and from Canada much easier. We couldn't really blame her, but we were sad to see her go. We wrapped up the millennium as empty nesters and the opportunity to create a new chapter. We just weren't sure at the time what we wanted it to look like.

Greatest lesson from Life #6

Expect the unexpected and learn how to adjust.

Greatest blessing from Life #6

A devoted partner and loving family.

REFLECTION

1. Think back to your life between ages fifty through fifty-nine. Can you recall any significant moments?

_____

_____

_____

_____

_____

2. What lessons did you learn from those experiences?

_____

_____

_____

_____

_____

3. What blessings did you receive from those experiences?

_____

_____

_____

_____

_____

4. Who was the most important person in your life at that time?

_____

_____

_____

_____

_____

5. What did you learn from them?

_____

_____

_____

_____

_____

6. Do you have someone in your life now who is that age whom you can support or mentor?

_____

_____

_____

_____

_____

7. How can you pay forward the lessons that you learned during that time?

_____

_____

_____

_____

_____

8. If you ARE this age now, what lessons from your past can you implement into your life now?

_____

_____

_____

_____

_____

Age three when we lived with my
grandparents in Baltimore.

Age five in Baltimore.

Age five with my Mother after she
married my Stepfather who was in
the Navy,

*Life#*7 RETIREMENT & LOSS

Life #7 began with welcoming the new millennium and the collective relief that we all survived transitioning to the year 2000. Leading up to January 1st, the conspiracy theories ran wild with all the crazy notions one could think of. The biggest was the Y2K scare around computers and how they wouldn't work properly if the system couldn't distinguish between 1900 and the year 2000. Luckily after everything I had experienced in my first sixty years, nothing surprised me anymore, and everything turned out to be okay.

As a family however, we faced some heartbreaking news as my father-in-law, Jose passed away. He was a dear man who lived a full life and passed away at age ninety-five. I'm so happy I had the opportunity to know him as he visited us from Peru. We'll always cherish those memories. It was an extremely difficult time for my wife as she was very close to her father and living so far apart didn't give her the chance to spend as much time with him in his older years as she would have hoped. For Cali, she was grateful for the two times she was able to visit Peru as a young child, and the time they spent together when he visited us here. Eric only visited Peru once but was too young to remember.

Luckily, he did get to know his grandfather when he spent time with us here.

My sixtieth birthday was pretty significant as I officially retired from working and focused on spending time with Bertha and enjoying our Golden years together. A few months later football was back in the headlines in Baltimore as the Baltimore Ravens won their first Super Bowl defeating the New York Giants 34-7 on January 28th. The first half of 2001 was spent rediscovering my love of art and creating my pen and ink drawings along with different novelty pieces I could sell at local markets. Since Bertha had a great relationship with the Catholic Church up from our home, we began to take part in their weekend flea markets where I could sell my artwork. The neighborhood and local markets became more frequent during the spring and summer months and I really enjoyed being out with the community and chatting with those who stopped by.

In July, 2001 a freight train derailed in the Howard Street tunnel and sparked a chemical fire that lasted for days and pretty much closed off downtown Baltimore. The derailment caused a major water main to burst flooding numerous streets and causing additional issues. Rail travel was halted and local businesses closed as the fire raged on for five days. Luckily we lived north of the downtown core and were not affected, but it sure was a mess. Also, luckily only five people experienced minor injuries.

The next big event was pretty life-altering. Cali had come down from New York to spend some time with us and Eric was also here when we woke to that horrifying news on the morning of September 11th. Our country was under attack by terrorists and the images we witnessed coming across the television screen were hard to comprehend. The attacks on the Twin Towers in New York City, the Pentagon in Washington, and the plane that went down in Pennsylvania, all senseless acts of terrorism. Nearly three thousand people died and no one really knew what to say as we looked on. The first thing to come to mind was my family and luckily we were all together and we were safe. The attacks sparked the Global War on Terrorism and thankfully I knew this was one war I wouldn't be a part of on the front line. It was a militant campaign initiated by the United States in response to the terrorist attacks and aimed at militant Islamist movements like Al-Qaeda, Taliban and their allies. Cali decided it was best to just stay in Baltimore for a while so she stayed for three additional weeks. It was nice having her with us and it eased our minds knowing she was okay.

2002 was another difficult year for us as a family, yet started off on a nice note as Cali had the opportunity to attend the Winter Olympic Games which were taking place in Salt Lake City, Utah. She had friends competing in both figure skating and ice hockey for Canada, and was there as part of the support crew for the Canadian Olympic Committee. Cali had dreamed of going to the Olympics ever since she was a little girl, so I was thrilled she was able to have that experience.

During the summer months she returned to Baltimore to spend time with us and my mother who lived nearby. Cali and her grandmother had a very special relationship and close bond. They did a lot together, including traveling together. Cali took her to San Diego and New York and just enjoyed spending time together. Little did we know that their time together would soon come to an end as my mother was diagnosed with colon cancer in October, 2002. She passed away on November 27th, the day before

Thanksgiving. The only comfort was that we had the whole family together for the holiday, so we were able to say goodbye surrounded by loved ones.

My mother's passing was more difficult than I thought it would be. Even though our relationship was strained when I was a child and young adult, we seemed to heal the wounds as time went by. Now I was all alone as both parents were no longer in my life. I had a choice to make in regards to my own children. What kind of father did I want to be? How could I be supportive, but also allow them to live their own lives? The holiday season of 2002 was a bit more special than in previous years as we came together as a family. With so much turmoil in the world and loss, we wanted to cherish every moment.

2003 began with more heartbreak and another war. On February 1st the Space Shuttle Columbia disintegrated after entering the atmosphere over Texas killing all seven astronauts onboard. Columbia had been in operation for twenty-two years and took part in twenty-eight missions for the Space Program. On March 20, 2003 the U.S. declared war on Iraq in hopes of disarming weapons of mass destruction, ending Saddam Hussein's support for terrorism, and freeing the Iraqi people.

In April of 2003 we visited Long Island, New York to spend time with Cali who had come down from Canada. We went to a hockey game to see the New York Islanders play and spent time checking out the sites and beauty of the island. 2003 also began a series of mishaps and more hospital visits. I came to realize I wasn't as limber as I had once been and it was taking more time to heal from my accidents. We had decided to get a dog some years back to keep us company since it was just the two of us more often. Boomer was the absolute best dog, so loyal and loving. However, I tended to take some spills when walking him. Towards the end of 2003 my wife began to question if he was too much to handle. Then in November I took a serious spill coming down the concrete stairs of the house with him. I hit my head and became disoriented. He sat by my side and barked for help. It was another hospital visit, but sadly the end of Boomer as well. I felt so bad for him as he was thirteen-years-old, but he had arthritis really bad and had developed other health problems. The vet told us the best thing we could do for him would be to put him down. It was the hardest thing we had to do and there were a lot of tears shed in our family that day and the days that followed.

The next few years I did my best to keep moving forward, but I was plagued by a number of health scares. The blows I had taken to my head led to me being in the hospital in 2004 with a brain aneurysm. I was lucky that it didn't rupture, but I was put on a serious rest prescription. I wasn't able to do anything strenuous and no traveling. I took the time to focus on my art and staying close to home. Then in 2007 I was diagnosed with prostate cancer. Luckily the diagnosis wasn't too serious and just recommended monitoring to make sure my numbers stayed where they needed to be. I also worked on changing my diet to include more fruits and vegetables as I was pretty much a junk food junkie. Still am really, but am open to trying new things.

In the summer of 2008 Cali had made the decision to move to California permanently. She had been spending more and more time there since 2002 and felt it was where she needed to be. She had a great job in New York and we were really proud of her, but this was something she really wanted to do. In October she decided she was going to drive across the country and asked her mother to join her. They would take nearly a month so they could enjoy everything our beautiful country has to offer. I stayed back in Baltimore as it was a bit too much on my system, but I was happy they could have this time together.

Each day I would receive a phone call about the day's activities and what they saw and experienced. They traveled over forty-two hundred miles taking in some incredible sites and experiences, from an architecture cruise in Chicago and visiting Wrigley Field, to visiting Mount Rushmore and feeding donkeys and seeing wild bison in Custer State Park. From the Garden of the Gods in Colorado to the Grand Canyon. From Las Vegas and Lake Tahoe to finally the Golden Gate in San Francisco. They saw it all. Cali knew the importance and significance of this trip even if my wife didn't realize it at the time. When they reached the Bay Area and settled into Cali's new home, she took her mother to the Golden Gate Bridge and encouraged her to walk across it together. At first Bertha was hesitant as they started on the San Francisco side, but she went along. When she reached the other side she called and was quite emotional. Cali said she had tears in her eyes and couldn't fully express the beauty and feelings she had after she made the trek. I was so happy she got to experience that.

In 2009 it was back to the hospital again and this time I was really getting tired of the frequent visits. This visit was certainly unexpected, but also a blessing in disguise. My wife and I were looking after my son's cat. All of the sudden the cat became very agitated and scratched my wife's leg. I reacted in surprise and went towards it to make sure it wouldn't scratch her again. All of the sudden it swiped at my leg and then lunged at my left hand, its teeth embedded in the wrist area. I was finally able to pry it away and lock it in the bathroom where we would be protected. When the ambulance came and we explained what had happened, they sent someone to get the cat to test it for rabies. Luckily it was clean in that area, but they discovered the poor cat had a cancerous tumor in its brain, thus the unexpected behavior. It was put down. It was such a traumatic experience, but we were at least happy the cat didn't have to suffer anymore.

That incident would leave a scar that would shape the next decade and deeply affect my artwork. During the surgery on my wrist and hand, the doctors accidently hit a nerve which left my pinky finger and side of my hand numb. I had real trouble making a fist and I wasn't able to draw anymore since it was my dominant hand. However, that was also a blessing in disguise. One day as I was out to lunch with my son, I made a comment about one of the bottle caps off his beer bottle. It was a local brand that had a stylish looking cap. I kept it and thought perhaps I could create a novelty using the cap. That one cap launched a whole new venture for me as I started collecting caps and attaching them to strings of beads, keychains, and earrings. As another decade ended, a new venture began.

Greatest lesson from Life #7

There's always a blessing in every difficult situation.

Greatest blessing from Life #7

My imagination.

REFLECTION

1. Think back to your life between ages sixty through sixty-nine. Can you recall any significant moments?

_____

_____

_____

_____

_____

2. What lessons did you learn from those experiences?

_____

_____

_____

_____

_____

3. What blessings did you receive from those experiences?

_____

_____

_____

_____

_____

4. Who was the most important person in your life at that time?

_____

_____

_____

_____

_____

5. What did you learn from them?

_____

_____

_____

_____

_____

6. Do you have someone in your life now who is that age whom you can support or mentor?

_____

_____

_____

_____

_____

7. How can you pay forward the lessons that you learned during that time?

_____

_____

_____

_____

_____

8. If you ARE this age now, what lessons from your past can you implement into your life now?

_____

_____

_____

_____

_____

Age ten after we moved to West
Baltimore.

Age 11 with my dog, Inky

Age seventeen when we lived in Waverly.

*Life#*8 LOCKDOWN & HEARTBREAK

Life #8 brought about an interesting time for all of us as a family. The medical bills were piling up between my wife and myself as many ailments weren't covered by insurance. We realized we could no longer simply enjoy retirement. We needed to be cautious of how we spent every dime. Cali decided to go to graduate school at the University of San Francisco in early 2009 on a partial scholarship, and launched an art career when one of her photographs was chosen to be exhibited as part of the Sausalito Art Festival.

For her mother's birthday in March, 2010 she flew Bertha out to the Bay Area for some mother/daughter time. They spent time enjoying the Bay and also visited Scottsdale, Arizona for a few days to take in Spring Training for the San Francisco Giants. Cali had begun following the Giants in 2002 during their World Series meeting with the Angels, and was fortunate enough to land an internship with the team during her time at USF. The Scottsdale trip was a wonderful experience for both of them as they reconnected with long-time friend, Cal Ripken, Jr. who was making the rounds at the different camps. It was a wonderful surprise for all of them.

Cali had also started her own event management company while in graduate school, but was having trouble securing new clients due to the plunging economy. She graduated from USF at the end of 2010 and sadly we weren't in a position to go to California for her graduation. I was told flying wasn't the best idea with my head injuries and we simply didn't have the funds. Eric was living his own life and doing what he could to be there, but it was really a difficult time for all of us.

Occupy Baltimore began in October, 2011 as a growing concern over the shortage of jobs, student loan debt and frustration over the economy. There were several Occupy events around the country with protestors voicing their concerns. We also experienced quite a jolt a couple months earlier when a 5.8 earthquake struck in nearby Virginia. It was one of the strongest to be felt in Maryland since the 1940s. I remember one when the children were young that had the lamp on the nightstand sway. This one was quite the jolt.

Between 2011 and 2013 the strain in our family dynamic grew. Cali was having a really difficult time simply getting by and as much as we would have welcomed her to come back to Baltimore, we all knew she wouldn't be happy here. She had been trying to find a way to leave for many years, even joking when she was young that the stork made a mistake and placed her in the wrong city. Eric on the other hand was a true Baltimorean from Day One who loved his Orioles and Ravens, and with whom we could enjoy a good crab dinner. He moved around a lot to different places here in Maryland, but we always knew he would be close by.

At the end of 2013 Cali decided to move to Los Angeles as life in the Bay Area became too expensive and she wasn't happy there anymore. Before long she had settled nicely in Santa Monica, met a fine young man, and was happy working with her creative projects. We couldn't have been happier, even if she was still on the other side of the country. She had invited us to move to California a number of times. I was always ready to go with one foot out the door. My wife on the other hand was always reluctant. She had her oldest friends and doctors here and couldn't imagine having to start over some place new. Therefore we stayed in Baltimore.

In 2015 we began to wonder if that was the best decision as the City became the center of unrest and uproar. It all began when a twenty-five-year-old African American named Freddie Gray died while in police custody. Protests began soon after his death and escalated over the course of a two-week period in April and May, 2015 with businesses vandalized, car and building fires, and looting. The National Guard was called in to support the police department in hopes of preventing the violence from escalating any further. It was certainly a scary time to be in Baltimore.

By 2017 Baltimore had recorded its highest homicide rate of nearly three hundred fifty killings. The Opioid epidemic raged as well. By 2018, Eric had had enough of Baltimore as well. We never thought he would leave, but the chaos of the last few years would be enough to give anyone second thoughts about calling Baltimore home. He decided North Carolina's beach towns were better suited for him moving forward. Initially, he had planned to move to Northern California and Cali was thrilled because she thought if they were both on the West Coast, it might finally entice us to move there as well. We did give it some serious thought, and I was certainly onboard, but again, we remained in Baltimore.

By 2019 my wife's health was beginning to take a turn for the worse. She had a number of issues including Sjögren's syndrome which is a chronic autoimmune disease. It causes the body's moisture-producing glands to be attacked by the immune system resulting in dry eyes and mouth. She had been using daily drops for her eyes, but her eye sight began to really decline. It was a crucial issue as she had been the one to do all the paperwork and pay the bills. Now she was having trouble reading the small print. Luckily Cali offered to help by handling the paperwork and paying the bills remotely from California. It was something we no longer had to worry about and that was a huge relief.

When the Covid pandemic struck in 2020, everything changed for us. We no longer left the house except for short stints to the grocery store or for doctor's appointments. The flea markets and events where I loved sharing my artwork no longer took place. Cali came to stay for a month in May which was so nice. She helped us organize all of our paperwork and finances. She made sure we had everything we needed and was there as Bertha and I celebrated our fiftieth wedding anniversary. Cali captured beautiful photos of us together and made a collage of photos beginning with our wedding day through the present. It was wonderful. We were so happy to be able to share that special time with her.

The seclusion and not being able to connect with friends and family took its toll as the year went by and by the time 2021 rolled around, my wife's health had severely declined. It only got worse in 2022 and by the time 2023 rolled around she was bedridden.

She could no longer go up and down the stairs of our Baltimore home, so we opened up one of the sleeper-sofas in the living room, and that is where she slept. After a while it became apparent that she would need assistance in the middle of the night so I turned the other sleeper-sofa into my own bed. That is where we slept for all of 2023 as I became her twenty-four, seven caretaker.

There were times when I didn't feel I could carry on. I was exhausted and every day became a repeat of the prior. My wife was on a cocktail of drugs and I had the schedule which ran from the time we woke until midnight. I barely slept. Cali expressed her concern and urged us to come to California, but by this point it was too late. Somehow Bertha knew this would be her final year on earth. She told us when the year began that this was it. We did everything we could to make her comfortable, but it was no way to live. It broke my heart to see her like that. She used to be so vibrant, so active and loved life. Now she was ready to go.

At the beginning of November, Cali told us that she was going to travel for a while, but that she was going to be on the east coast and would stop by to spend some time with us. We were thrilled. After spending a couple weeks in New York City, she came down to Baltimore for a week and to celebrate our birthdays early as she had to return to Los Angeles for work before heading to San Diego for Thanksgiving. It was wonderful to have her with us. She helped out a lot and I was finally able to take a break and rest a bit. On November 15th she kissed her mother goodbye and reminded her that she would be back in January. She then headed back to L.A.

While she was in San Diego on our birthday we had a wonderful conversation and wished one another a happy birthday. The next day began pretty much how all the previous ones had, waking and helping Bertha with her needs, making sure she took her prescriptions, and then watching her drift off to sleep as I sat and watched TV. I talked to Cali on the phone after dinner and we had a nice chat. I told her Bertha looked so at peace and that it had been a good day. A couple hours later when I went to wake her to give her her medicine I realized she wasn't breathing. In a panic I called Cali. I'm not sure how she understood what I was saying as I didn't want to face the reality. The paramedics arrived and performed CPR but she was gone. My neighbor came and stayed with me and was truly a lifesaver. He and his wife are such good people and were there so many times over the course of the last year offering to get us groceries or whatever we needed. In the most painful moment of my life, they were there again. Cali spoke to the police officer and paramedics and made all the arrangements for the removal of the body. I was too numb to handle any of that. Luckily she had all of my wife's medical records and information, so everything went smoothly. It was nearly midnight by the time everyone left and I was alone. My neighbors assured me that if I needed anything they were just next door.

Cali was on the first flight out of San Diego the following morning and arrived in Baltimore around 4:00 pm. Eric arrived later that night and it meant the world to me to have my children with me. I'm not sure how I would have survived without them and my neighbors. My entire life had shattered and I had no idea how I would carry on.

Greatest lesson from Life #8

Life is so fragile and we must cherish every moment.

Greatest blessing from Life #8

Fifty-three beautiful years with the love of my life.

REFLECTION

1. Think back to your life between ages seventy through eighty-two. Can you recall any significant moments?

_____

_____

_____

_____

_____

2. What lessons did you learn from those experiences?

_____

_____

_____

_____

_____

3. What blessings did you receive from those experiences?

_____

_____

_____

_____

_____

4. Who was the most important person in your life at that time?

_____

_____

_____

_____

_____

5. What did you learn from them?

_____

_____

_____

_____

_____

6. Do you have someone in your life now who is that age whom you can support or mentor?

_____

_____

_____

_____

_____

7. How can you pay forward the lessons that you learned during that time?

_____

_____

_____

_____

_____

8. If you ARE this age now, what lessons from your past can you implement into your life now?

_____

_____

_____

_____

_____

With Mom and Grandma as I
left for Basic Training 1966.

Vietnam Service reminders

Bertha & I and our first
home together, 1977.

Bertha & I celebrating our 50th
wedding anniversary 2020.

With Cali on our way to Los
Angeles, March 2024.

Life #9 DREAMS REIGNITED & STARTING OVER

Life #9 began in a heart wrenching state of grief. The days following my wife's passing were pretty much a blur. I felt as if I was just going through the motions, stopping every now and then as the tears filled my eyes knowing I'd never see her again. I began to question everything. What do I do now? How do I carry on? What is my purpose for being here? There were no answers. I felt lost and alone. The one constant in my life over the course of the last fifty-three years was gone. How could I possibly move forward without her?

Thanksgiving Day came and it was bittersweet. Cali and Eric did everything they could to help lighten the mood. We had a nice dinner and watched "Home Alone" and the San Francisco Forty-Niners win. Cali made all the arrangements for the burial. I didn't want a funeral as I didn't feel I could handle being surrounded by a lot of people. I also wanted to remember her in my own way. Bertha didn't have life insurance so we had to come up with the funeral costs on our own. Cali took care of everything and assured me not to worry. Everything was being taken care of and I could solely focus on my grieving.

At one point it all seemed to be too much. I sat on the sofa in tears when Cali sat down beside me. She was about to give me a

75

good talking to, something at the time I didn't realize I needed, but it changed everything. She shared how much she loved the man in her life and how much they had shared together over the last decade, but that they each had their own lives, their own dreams, and their own purpose for being here on earth. She shared that as much as she loved him, she knew that her life mattered just as much, as did mine. She assured me that I was allowed to grieve in any way I needed to, for as long as I needed to, and that it would be okay. She assured me that she would be there for support and to take care of all the logistics. All I needed to do was find the will to carry on. I knew she was right, even though the pain seemed unbearable at the time.

December rolled around and Cali was making preparations to head back to L.A. She needed to get back but left me with a list of things I could do to keep me occupied and support me with the healing process. She also called every day so we could stay in touch. She would be back in January and Eric was planning to come and spend Christmas with me. The next major step was selling the house after forty-seven years. I never thought that would happen either. I always figured I'd die in that house, but apparently God had other plans.

Cali assured me she would take care of that as well. She had been referred to a realtor here in Baltimore by an L.A. friend/realtor and made the connection while she was here. The first thing we needed to do was declutter the house and that was one heck of a project since Bertha kept everything. When Cali was here in November she actually began the process by consolidating all the photographs that were in multiple photo albums into one box. She left me with the task of going through my personal items and deciding what I wanted to keep and what I wanted to toss and donate. I was happy to have something to do to keep my mind off my loss.

2024 began with a feeling of hope. I was still grieving the loss of my wife, but I also took to heart what Cali had shared in my darkest hour. I knew there must be a greater purpose for my life even if I didn't have any idea what that could be. I knew I needed to take things one day at a time and keep moving forward. What I didn't share earlier was the visit I had from my beautiful Bertha the first two days after she passed. That first night without her I decided to sleep in her bed so I could feel close to her. She came to me and I could feel her presence. It was like a blow of a soft breeze, but I felt loved. The next day I saw her as a white mist and then she softly kissed my cheek. I knew she was finally at peace. No more suffering. That made me feel a bit better.

Cali came back to Baltimore the second week of January for another five weeks. During this time the main objective was the decluttering of the house and only keeping what was absolutely necessary. We also met with the realtor, Michelle who was a dream to work with. She was very compassionate about the situation and understood the significance of selling the family home and moving cross-country. She made everything feel effortless and we were grateful for her support. We had everything in the house organized and all of my personal belongings we planned to take to L.A in a local storage unit. We made the house presentable so photographs could be taken and the house was listed for sale on February 5th. It felt like a huge weight had been lifted, but we knew it was also just the beginning.

On February 10th Cali headed back to L.A. and would return in early March. On February 12th she called me to let me know she had received an all-cash offer on the house. Things were moving faster than expected. I had mixed feelings at first about selling the house, but knew it was the right decision in the end. I couldn't stay here by myself. Neither Cali nor Eric wanted to live in Baltimore, and Cali assured me California was the answer. It was difficult as I felt it was yet another loss, my first real home, a house I had purchased on my own, now going as well. At times the feelings were a bit overwhelming, but I knew I needed to carry on.

Cali arrived back in Baltimore on March 5th, what would have been my wife's eighty-fifth birthday. She knew it would be a difficult day and made it special simply by being here. Each day was filled with the final decluttering of leftover items. There was so much and it wasn't easy. There came a point where we both realized if it was meant for us to have it, we would. We simply needed to let go of the rest. On March 12th the realtor and representative from the title company came so we could sign all the paperwork. The closing date was March 19th and we were heading to Los Angeles on the 14th, so the final details needed to be completed remotely. Luckily that wasn't a problem and everything went smoothly. Eric and his girlfriend came up from North Carolina for a few days to help and we were grateful for that. We also had some local friends help as well. It was a lot of work so the more the merrier.

March 14, 2024 – A new chapter begins. It started off on a bit of a rocky note on the flight to L.A., but somehow I managed to get through it. I hadn't been on a plane in decades and I'm not very comfortable in confined places. Also, I had only about three hours of sleep and hadn't eaten much. About four hours into the trip I began to feel lightheaded and my legs were going numb. Cali gestured to the flight attendant that I needed some oxygen and the Southwest crew jumped into action. Luckily there was also a Baltimore-based doctor sitting a few rows from us who came over to help. Cali explained what was happening and she ended up doing some tests, blood pressure, etc. All the numbers were good. I really just needed to walk around a bit and get the blood flowing properly. We landed safely in Baltimore and everyone was so kind offering well-wishes as we deplaned. Cali's friend Lisa was there to pick us up and drive us to Santa Monica. She took the beach route so I can get a glimpse of the ocean and the life that awaited me.

The next three weeks were spent house/kitty-sitting for Cali's friends in Santa Monica. They loved to travel and it was nice to have a place for an extended period of time while we looked for our new home. Cali had put all of her belongings in storage as she had planned to travel for a year, so we were looking for a new home that we would share. She wanted us to remain in Santa Monica as that is where the core of her friends lived and it was a beautiful place to live. Each day since arriving in L.A. was an adventure. Cali took me everywhere and each day was different and special. She introduced me to friends and showed me so many beautiful places. One very special day came when we woke early enough to walk down to the beach to watch the sunrise, and then also had the opportunity to watch it set over the Ocean. Cali took photos and video of the sunset and we discovered something quite remarkable. We noticed a red orb in each of the sunset photos, but in the video the orb changed shape and you could see what appeared to be an angel spreading its wings. I knew in that moment it was my beautiful wife letting me know she was there, and that she was okay.

We visited so many great places and even ventured to other parts of L.A. Another special moment came when we went to Hollywood and saw the film, "Mary Poppins" at the El Capitan Theatre on Hollywood Blvd. I had seen the film many times on television and on VHS and DVD, but never in the theatre, so that was very special. We also got to meet one of the theatre workers who struck up a conversation. We left feeling so great about enjoying the film together as well as making a new friend. The next day Cali took me to my very first chiropractic appointment. She has been going to the chiropractor for years and thought I would benefit. I wasn't sure what to expect, but I was open to the new experience. Well, I was very pleased with the outcome. I walked out of the office feeling like a new person and the doctor was great. He took the time to really listen to my concerns and carefully adjusted my neck and spinal column. I was grateful for the experience as I know how important it is to look after my health.

That evening Cali took me to the Santa Monica Pier for Locals' Night. It was great as they had a nice collection of classic cars lined up on the Pier and I got to see my dream car, a 1957 Chevy Bel Air. We had dinner at a great restaurant and watched the sunset over the Ocean again. The first couple of weeks were nonstop sightseeing. We headed back to Hollywood one weekend to meet up with Cali's filmmaker friends at the Academy of Motion Pictures Museum. We met the group for a late lunch at Fanny's and I ate the most delicious hamburger I've ever had in my life. Then we toured the museum and the memories of the classic films were great. There was so much to see. We all took a group photo with Oscar and everyone was so warm and welcoming. They made me feel right at home. In fact, everyone I met made me feel that way, and I was grateful the transition was smooth.

We looked at a few apartments in the area, but nothing felt right. Either there was only one bedroom and we required two, or the price was out of our set budget. We were also coming up against an obstacle in that every place we visited wanted three month's rent as income and we simply didn't have that. We even offered to pay six months in advance, but no one would go for that. It became frustrating after a while, but Cali assured me that we would end up in the perfect place when the time was right.

After the three weeks we spent in Santa Monica, Cali suggested we take a week's holiday and go down to San Diego. She lived in North County for a couple years during the pandemic and said that I may like it. The day we planned to head to San Diego was also the Total Solar Eclipse on April 8th. As we walked to get the rental car, Cali spotted a white fuzzy dandelion on the ground. She picked it up and said, "Let's make a wish!" We wished to find the perfect home where we could live out this next chapter in our lives and together we blew the petals off. The very next day our dream came true.

We stayed in Encinitas and had rented a car for the week. She took me to all her favorite places such as Coronado Island, La Jolla, and Carlsbad. We saw so many beautiful places and every day felt like a dream. We looked at another apartment in a great complex in Encinitas, but came across the same issue of three times the rent in income. Cali then suggested we try a place in Oceanside that she had discovered when she lived there before.

She called and we were invited to visit the complex. We met with the property manager and learned they had a two-bedroom unit coming available in May. We asked about their policy when it came to income and they assured us we would be fine just paying the standard one-month's rent along with the security deposit. We were thrilled and secured the apartment. It had everything we wanted, gated community, two-bedrooms, two baths, pool, fitness center and steps from the Ocean. It even came with an Ocean view from our bedrooms which never gets old.

After our weeks' vacation in San Diego and securing our new home, we returned to L.A. and stayed at another friend's home for three more weeks. This place was in Hollywood and we had access to her car as well which was great. Cali continued to show me around and we visited so many more stunning places such as El Matador State Beach and Point Dume in Malibu. We also spent time at The Griffith Observatory and Griffith Park which I really enjoyed. We took Day Trips to Newport Beach and San Pedro where we visited the Marine Mammal Rehabilitation Center. We wrapped up the month of April by renting a U-Haul truck and moving all of Cali's belongings that she had stored in L.A. down to San Diego. This would make it easier once we were able to move into our new home in May.

Our official move-in date was not set in stone as the current tenant was still living there and they had to do some refurbishing once they moved out. We didn't mind. We were able to secure pet-setting opportunities in both North County and back in L.A. through the first two weeks of June. That way we could slowly move our things in when we were in San Diego and begin furnishing our new home while we also had a place to sleep elsewhere. It all worked out so perfectly and we were grateful for everyone who supported us during this time. At the beginning of June while we were staying in Hollywood, Cali flew back to Baltimore and made the arrangements to have my belongings that were in storage there shipped out to California now that we had a home.

By the middle of June we were finally able to move fully into our new seaside home and I was thrilled. As much as I enjoyed all the experiences of traveling from place to place and everything we saw and got to experience over the course of the last three months, I was ready to put down roots again, and now we had a place to call a home of our own. My belongings from Baltimore arrived within the following week and we could finally begin to unpack and make our new place a home.

When it came to choosing what to bring from Baltimore, it was all about sentimental value and things I needed. Two items in particular were very special. The first was the dining set (circle table and two wooden chairs) that my wife and I purchased when we first got married. The other was a storage cabinet that I loved that housed dry food goods in our Baltimore home. Cali was happy to bring both but asked if I'd mind if she painted them and gave them a new life. At first I was a bit hesitant until she showed me photos of what she had in mind. I trusted her knowing how creative she is that they would turn out nicely, and I was right. They were better than I could have anticipated and look perfect in our new home.

The first item Cali purchased for me for our new home was a new art table complete with storage drawers and enclosed shelving below. It was so perfect and became my favorite spot in my room to create my artistic projects. We also have a garage which is currently being used for storage, but we're hoping to create a small art studio there as well. We have so many new dreams as we begin this next chapter. Everyone in the complex is so nice and have been so welcoming. We feel right at home already and I'm so glad.

Once we were a bit settled in at the beginning of July, Cali took me to the Veteran's Administration to finally get registered for benefits. Many years ago when I first came back from Vietnam I went to the VA in Maryland to see if I could apply for disability since I was still having trouble with my knee after surgery. It was such a bad experience and I felt completely overlooked that I refused to have anything to do with the VA from that point forward. Cali knew it was something that I needed and made sure I went when I came to California. Well, it was like night and day. We went to the VA in Oceanside and from the moment I walked through the door I was welcomed with open arms. Within a week I had my new card and was assigned a new primary doctor. I couldn't believe how easy it was, but I was sure grateful for the treatment.

Being in North County San Diego felt like we were meant to be there all along. Everyone we met was so nice and welcoming. We met new people every day as we walked everywhere or took public transportation. We spent a lot of time in neighboring Carlsbad and began to meet other artists. We learned about different art events around town and neighboring towns and became excited about the possibilities of sharing our work with our new community.

In the third week of July, Cali left for Paris, France to take in the Summer Olympic Games as part of the support crew for Team

Canada. As a figure skater, she skated for both the United State and Canadian figure skating associations, and in 2002 she supported the COC at the Winter Olympic Games in Salt Lake City. One of the reasons she wanted to find a place for us in Santa Monica was to know that I'd have friends close by while she traveled. Luckily, we had that at our new home in San Diego. Between the property manager who is a great guy and our neighbors, I was well looked after while she was away for those two weeks. Plus, my son Eric called daily so that was nice as well.

During the time Cali was in Paris I kept myself occupied with my art projects and taking my daily walks to the beach. Prior to leaving, Cali would walk with me every day so I grew to know the path and it became my favorite part of the day. She also left the fridge fully stocked so I didn't have to worry about food. It was nice as I continued to get to know my neighbors and learn more about our new neighborhood. Sitting on the bench overlooking the Ocean was the best. I could have stayed there all day. It became my favorite spot.

As each week passed I began to count them and then recall all the things I had seen and the people I had met. When Cali returned from Paris she decided to purchase a large scrapbook and create photo collages for each week dating back to when I first arrived in California. Each page contained a large square photo collage and then around the edges Cali placed ticket stubs, stickers and small mementos of the places we visited.

There were certainly some adjustments when Cali and I became roommates after twenty-five years apart. She likes to eat fresh organic foods and I'm a junk-food-junkie. I prefer my hotdogs, chocolate, Fritos and Pepsi. She likes Green Tea, fruits and spinach. She offered me a little of her Green Drink once. I humored her by taking a sip and I actually liked it. Then I asked her what was in it and that was enough for me to pass. I will admit I am doing better in eating more fruits and vegetables and drinking juices instead of soda. She still allows me to have my Pepsi, but now it's a treat on the weekends instead of every day. She also spoke to the doctor to make sure the medications I was taking are absolutely necessary. We were able to get rid of one I was taking for heartburn. Since I changed my diet, I'm not experiencing that anymore. I was also taking Acetaminophen for pain, but that resulted in a constant headache. Once I stopped taking that, they headaches went away. Now I'm focusing more on eating foods that fight inflammation instead of relying on over-the-counter drugs.

Since Cali and I are both artists, Cali decided to create a new brand for us to help promote our artwork and get our names out into the community. She came up with the name, THE MERMAID & THE VETERAN and created a new logo, table banner, and postcards. We joined the Carlsbad Oceanside Art League and began showing our work at local community events like the First Friday Art Walk in Oceanside and the Art-on-the-Green weekend shows in Carlsbad. Back in February while we were still in Baltimore, we had a meeting with our realtor and I began sharing stories of my childhood. Cali looked at me and said, "How are you still alive" and we laughed thinking I was a cat with nine lives. Thus the title of this book and the moment this idea of writing a book was berthed. Once we were settled into our new home, Cali sat me down at the table with her camera set up and recorded answers to questions about my life. Those stories have now become the book you are holding in your hands. I hope you're enjoying it.

September and October were filled with beautiful days. Each day we would take a walk, either down to our favorite perch overlooking the Ocean or to some place new nearby. Another favorite spot has been the walking path along Carlsbad State Beach and Tamarack Beach. We walk along the path and stop to gaze up at the pelican that glide in massive numbers or skim the water above the surfers as they look to catch the perfect wave. We've come to know the resident California Falcon who Cali named Fred. He has his favorite perch atop a tree in front of our home or sometimes we see him being chased by crows as they look to protect their territory. Cali has captured some incredible photographs of him and he's quite stunning.

We've run into rabbits and squirrels, lizards and butterflies, and then the hummingbirds who visit us daily. Ever since we moved into our new home, a hummingbird comes and sits in the tree outside of Cali's bedroom window. Every single day it is there and it's quite remarkable. The weather has been wonderful, sunshine and blue skies, not too hot. It's perfect. My health has improved so much and I feel more like I'm in my sixties rather than eighty-four. I'm grateful for all that has come into my life over the course of the last year, and I'm excited to see what the future holds.

I look back to that first week and how desperately my heart ached. I had no idea what the future would look like without my beautiful wife. I didn't feel I deserved to move forward without her. Now I realize that she's always with me and she always will be. There have been moments when I can feel her presence and sense her looking down upon us smiling at what we have created together. I feel as though I now have a new lease on life and the sky's the limit. Anything is possible. It's never too late to start over and I'm living proof you can create a life you truly love if you simply take that first step.

If you're currently sitting in this place of uncertainty, not knowing what the future holds, it's okay. You'll never know how strong you are, or what you are capable of, unless you too take that first step. I believe in you. You can do this.

Greatest lesson from Life #9

It's never too late to start over if you're willing to try.

Greatest blessing from Life #9

The opportunity to wake up each day and do what I love, and the knowing that I'm never alone.

REFLECTION

1.   Think back to your life between ages eighty-three through present day. Can you recall any significant moments?

_____

_____

_____

_____

_____

2. What lessons did you learn from those experiences?

_____

_____

_____

_____

_____

3. What blessings did you receive from those experiences?

_____

_____

_____

_____

_____

4. Who was the most important person in your life at that
    time?

_____

_____

_____

_____

_____

5. What did you learn from them?

_____

_____

_____

_____

_____

6. Do you have someone in your life now who is that age whom you can support or mentor?

_____

_____

_____

_____

_____

7. How can you pay forward the lessons that you learned during that time?

_____

_____

_____

_____

_____

8. If you ARE this age now, what lessons from your past can you implement into your life now?

_____

_____

_____

_____

_____

ABOUT THE AUTHORS

Joseph Gilbert is a retired United States Army and Air Force veteran who served in both Vietnam and Desert Storm. A life-long artist, Joe is passionate about sharing his creations with the world. After losing his wife of 53 years in 2023, Joe moved to California with his daughter, Cali and began a new chapter at age 83. Joe is excited about the journey that lies ahead. As an artist, Joe focuses on creating pen and ink drawings of various subjects for both adults and children. He also enjoys abstract painting and creating novelties using unconventional materials. The novelties come with a seaside theme and also for the holidays.

Cali Gilbert is a ten-time international bestselling author, two-time award winning filmmaker, photographer, and social entrepreneur. As a former figure skater and magazine publisher, with an extensive background in event management, Cali has supported many global events including the 2002 Winter Olympic Games in Salt Lake City, Utah, the 34th America's Cup sailing regatta in San Francisco in 2013, and the 2024 Paris Summer Olympic Games.

In 2012 Cali created the *IT'S SIMPLY Series* of books and has published several books of her own along with supporting new authors. Cali is also an inspirational speaker for women's groups and supports creatives via her nonprofit, **Tower 15 Productions** in the areas of publishing, photography and filmmaking. Cali splits her time between Los Angeles and San Diego, California.

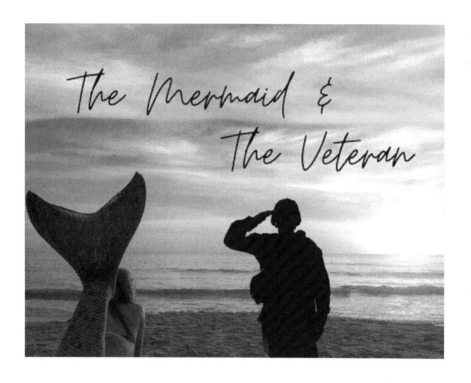

To learn more about Joe and how he is currently
sharing his artwork with the world, visit

www.Tower15Productions.com/mermaidandveteran

Other books by Cali Gilbert

It's Simply...Sausalito: An Inspirational Journey
ISBN-13 978-1467924436
ISBN-10 1467924431

It's Simply...GOLDEN: 75 Years of Inspiration
ISBN-13 978-1467903615
ISBN-10 1467903612

It's Simply...SF: Our City by the Bay
ISBN-13 978-1469969282
ISBN-10 1469969289

It's Simply SAILING: Our Voyage to the 2013 America's Cup
ISBN-13 978-1475108910
ISBN-10 1475108915

It's Simply Serendipity: Four Steps to Manifesting a Life of Bliss
ISBN-13 978-1475195538
ISBN-10 1475195532

It's Simply Publishing: Step by Step Guide to Writing, Marketing
& Publishing Your First Book
ISBN-13 978-1497488274
ISBN-10 1497488273

PEARL: A Guide to Living an Authentic & Purposeful Life
ISBN-13 978-1503031098
ISBN-10 1503031098

TIMING THE TIDES: A Tale of Love Sparked on the Titanic,
Rekindled a Century Later
ISBN-13 978-1535035729
ISBN-10 1535035722

IT'S SIMPLY FILMMAKING
ISBN-10 1986062414
ISBN-13 978-1986062411

PERCEPTION
ISBN-13 9781545042175

SHUFFLING THE TIDES
ISBN-13 978-1798941348

THE MANIFESTING MERMAID: 8 Steps Towards Creating
Money, Magic & Massive Success
ISBN: 9798860464124

.

Made in the USA
Columbia, SC
20 November 2024

47039190R00057